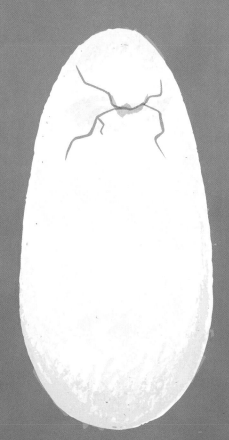

Here is a **LIFESIZE** Allosaurus footprint,
put your foot on top and see whose is
the biggest! Allosaurus could run up to
55 kilometres per hour, which makes it
one of the fastest dinosaurs **EVER**.

First published in Great Britain 2019 by Red Shed,
an imprint of Egmont UK Limited
2 Minster Court, London EC3R 7BB
www.egmont.co.uk

Text and illustrations copyright © Sophy Henn 2019
Sophy Henn has asserted her moral rights.
ISBN 978 1 4052 9395 2
68532/003
Printed in China
Consultancy by Professor Mike Benton.
A CIP catalogue record for this book is available from the British Library.

LIFESIZE

Sophy Henn

DINOSAURS

and Prehistoric Creatures

RED SHED

Dinosaurs roamed this planet a long, long, loooong time ago (between 252-66 million years ago in fact), so sadly we can't pop to a zoo to see them. That makes it tricky to picture just how big a T. rex's smile was . . .

Tricky, but not impossible! Every time you see the word **LIFESIZE** in this book, you will know you are looking at a dinosaur or part of a dinosaur that is actual size.

So come on! Let's go on a **LIFESIZE** adventure and see how you measure up against some of the smallest and **LARGEST** dinosaurs and prehistoric creatures.

This is a **LIFESIZE** Microraptor – one of the smallest dinosaurs we know of. Although he had wings, he couldn't fly! Instead he would glide from tree to tree looking for a tasty lizard to eat. YUM!

Let's start at the very beginning . . .
dinosaurs began their lives as eggs!
And those eggs came in different shapes,
sizes and colours, just like these **LIFESIZE**
dinosaur eggs . . .

WOW! This **LIFESIZE**
Beibeilong egg is the largest
known dinosaur egg **EVER**.

This **LIFESIZE** Deinonychus
egg is hatching – awwwww,
how cute! But not for long,
as this little dino grew up
into a deadly predator!

Quite possibly the smallest dinosaur
egg is this **LIFESIZE** Massospondylus egg.
But Massospondylus wasn't the smallest
dinosaur ever – see how big it grew
at the back of this book!

This **LIFESIZE** Diplodocus egg would have been laid in the forest and then covered with earth and leaves. Once the baby hatched, it would push up through the earth and have to fend for itself straight away.

Here is a **LIFESIZE** Maiasaura egg – the baby dino inside was up to 30 centimetres long and curled up into a tight ball to fit inside the egg.

OUCH! This **LIFESIZE** Utahraptor's claw looks super sharp. Hold your foot up to the page and see how it would look on you!

Utahraptors had a claw on each foot that curled up at a sharp angle so it didn't touch the ground when they walked along. This kept it super sharp for hunting, which was something raptors were really, really, REALLY good at.

Can you believe that among these deadly dinosaurs, millions of years ago, bees were buzzing about? The oldest bee found, trapped in amber, was 3 millimetres long and 100 million years old!

Gastonia had some of the best body armour of all the dinosaurs. It also had a spikey tail that came in very handy for fighting off predators, like these Utahraptors . . . watch out!

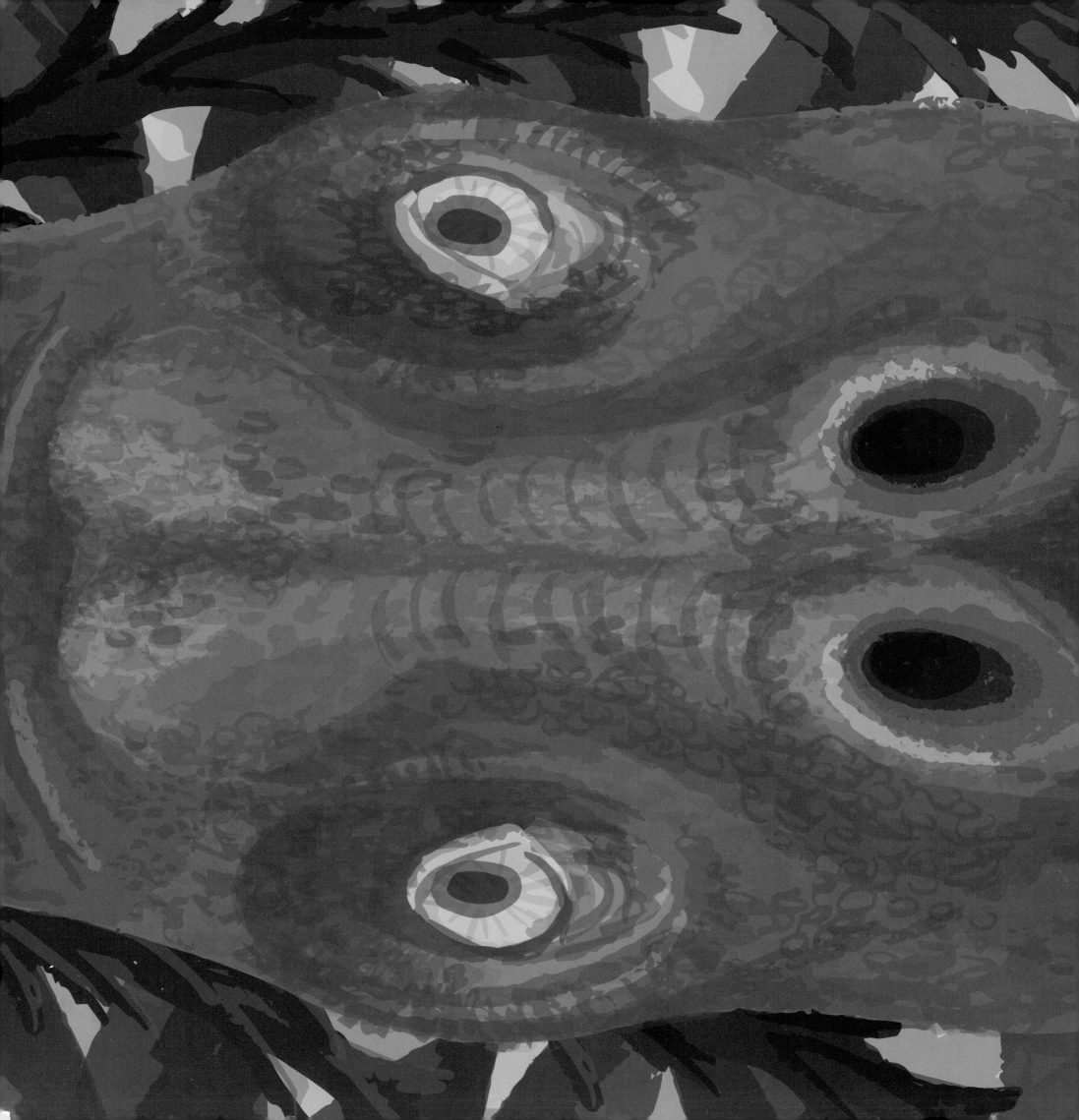

You are nose to **LIFESIZE** nose with a Diplodocus.
Can you flare your nostrils as big as his?

Diplodocus was one of the longest dinosaurs EVER. It had a **REALLY** long tail that it could whip at supersonic speeds, which made a **VERY** loud **BOOM**. It made this noise to scare away predators or to show off to other Diplodocus.

To be this completely GINORMOUS, Diplodocus had to eat A LOT. In fact, it had to eat so much that it didn't even have time to chew, so Diplodocus just gulped down its food instead.

Being so HUGE meant Diplodocus didn't
have to worry too much about predators,
but Allosaurus, with its super hunting skills,
was thought to have been its biggest threat.

How does this **LIFESIZE** Stegosaurus plate look on your back?

Imagine having 20 more like an actual Stegosaurus!

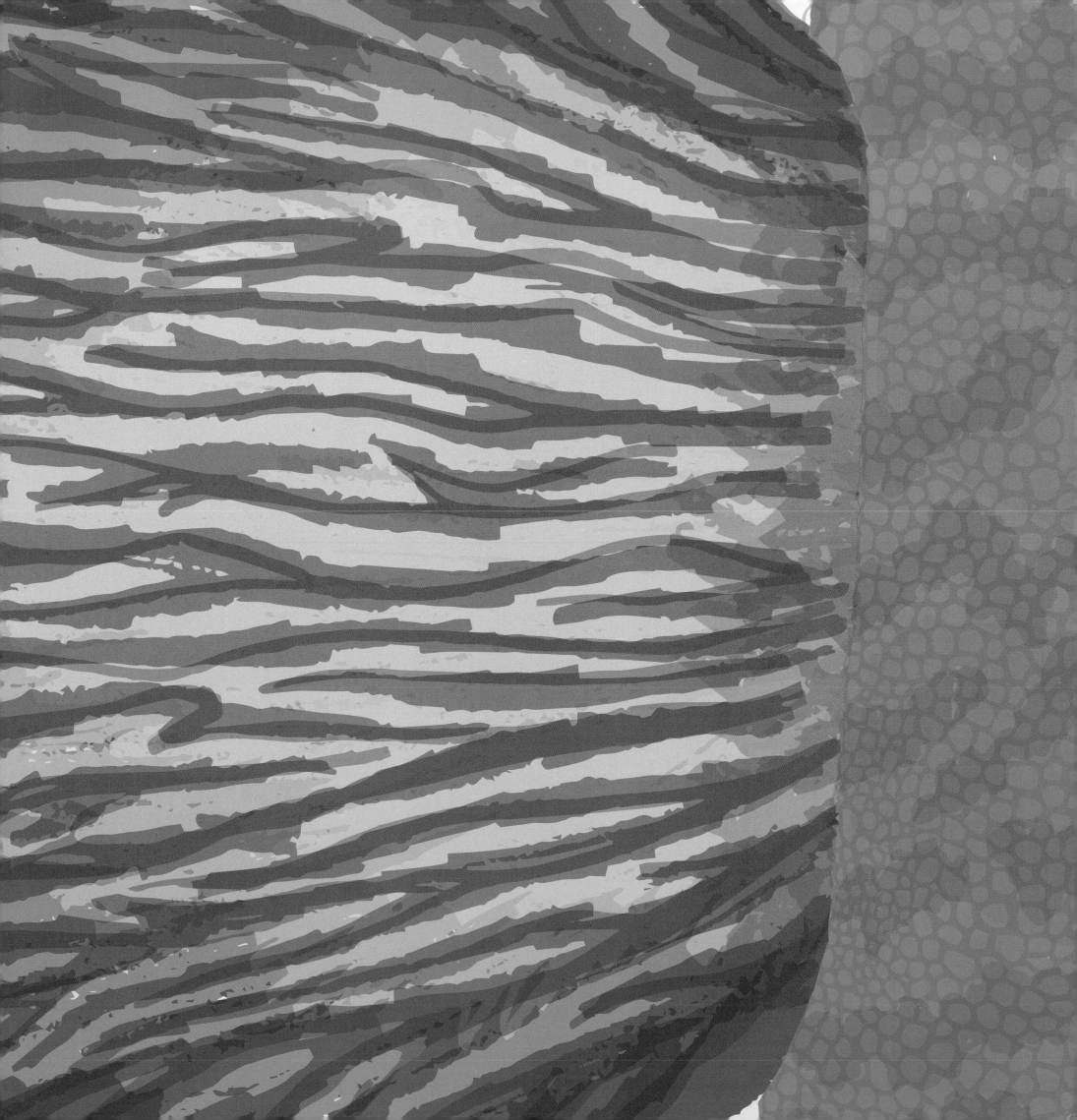

Stegosaurus was actually quite a snazzy dinosaur as it could change the colour of its back plates when it was competing for a mate or for territory.

Although it looked fancy, Stegosaurus wasn't so clever as its brain was only as big as a walnut.

Allosaurus was probably Stegosaurus' least favourite dinosaur as it had a habit of eating them! Allosaurus was a fearsome hunter with 70 serrated teeth and a really big mouth – all the better for biting with!

Isn't this **LIFESIZE** Pteranodon's beak HUGE?
Hold it up to the side of your nose and
see how it looks on you!

Pteranodon were not dinosaurs or birds, they were actually flying reptiles. They didn't have feathers but had wings made of stretched skin that they used for swooping and soaring.

Pteranodon would soar above the sea looking for fish, diving down to catch them in its beak.

This long-necked creature is an **Albertonectes.**
It was a plesiosaur, which isn't a dinosaur but a marine reptile. With such a long neck (about 7 metres), the Albertonectes could only swim very slowly and flapped it's flippers a bit like bird wings to propel itself forward.

ay cheese! See how your toothy grin compares to this **LIFESIZE** yrannosaurus rex's sneaky smile!

Tyrannosaurus rex might have been the most powerful land predator to have ever lived and had the **biggest teeth** of all the dinosaurs ever, but it couldn't stick its tongue out! T. rex's tongue was attached to the bottom of its mouth so it couldn't blow raspberries either!

Triceratops means 'Three-horned Face'. Its fancy neck frill was made of solid bone and most likely used for showing off to other Triceratops.

Although it was a favourite meal of T. rex, Triceratops was a plant eater and had up to 800 tiny teeth for cutting up leaves.

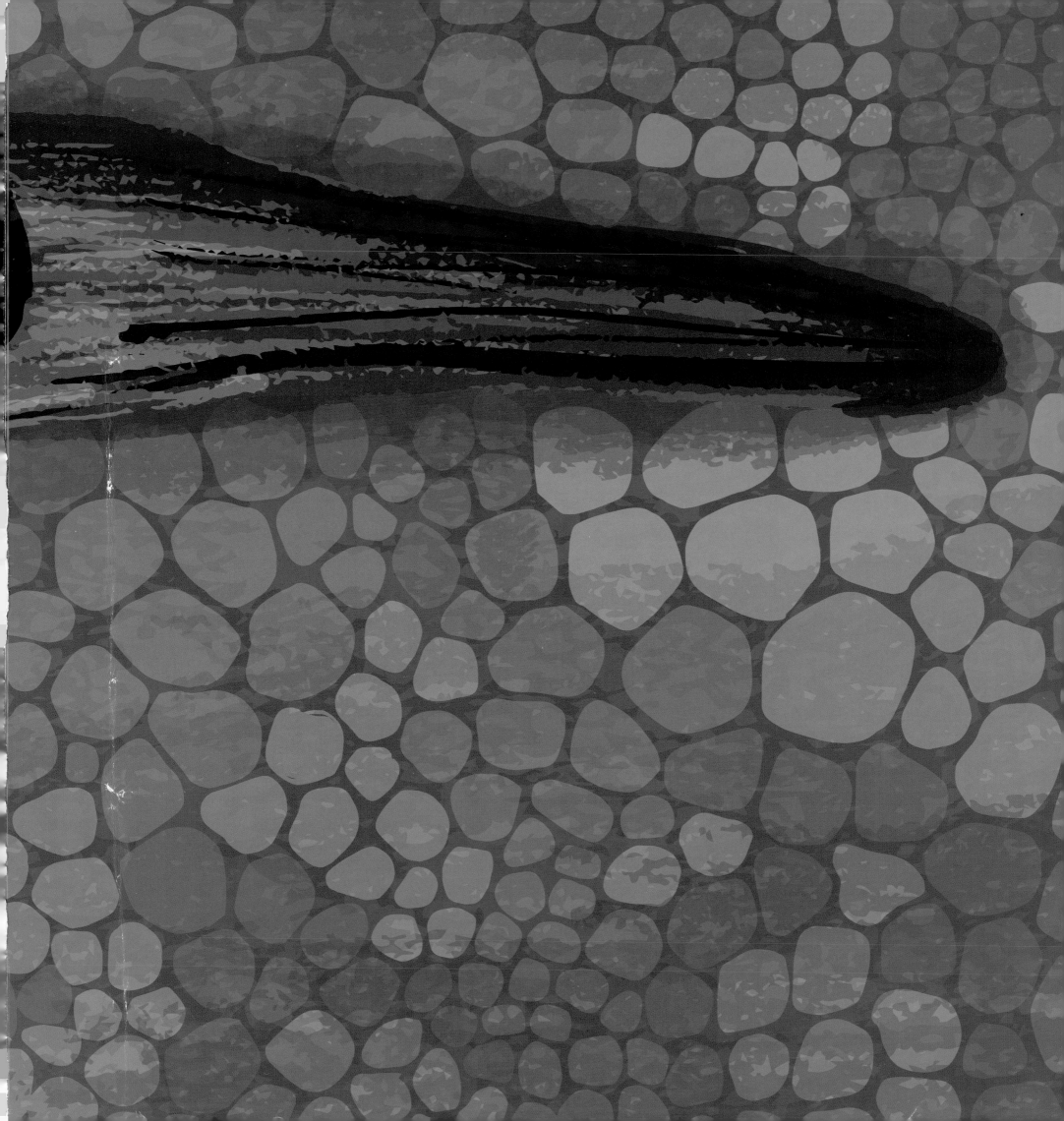

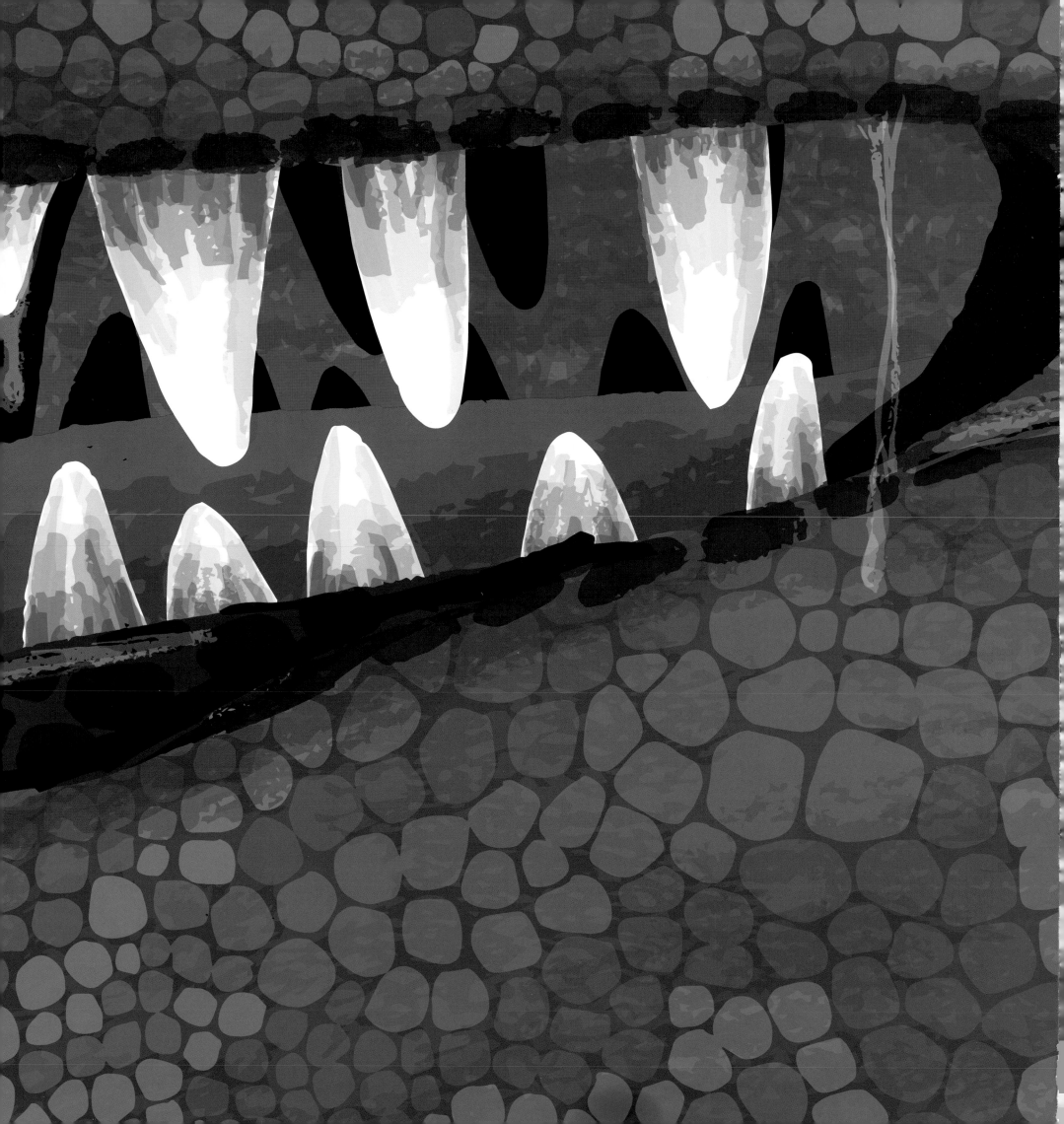

Wow! We've travelled back in time to see some amazing **LIFESIZE** dinosaurs and prehistoric creatures. Let's see how they compare in size to one another. And then measure yourself using the book to find out how you compare.

20 LIFESIZE books

Pteranodon (TEH-ran-oh-don)
Wingspan: up to 6 metres
Did you know? Pteranodon had a beautiful head crest that kept its head balanced and helped it steer when flying.

Diplodocus (dip-LOD-er-cus)
Head to tail: up to 25 metres
Did you know? Diplodocus never stopped growing throughout its whole life!

83 LIFESIZE books

Allosaurus (al-oh-SORE-us)
Head to tail: up to 8.5 metres
Did you know? An Allosaurus head was so big and heavy that if it hadn't had such a big tail it would have just fallen over!

Stegosaurus (steg-oh-SORE-us)
Head to tail: up to 9 metres
Did you know? Stegosaurus means 'roof lizard'.

30 LIFESIZE books

28 LIFESIZE books

Beibeilong (BAY-bay-long)

Head to tail: up to 8 metres

Did you know? Beibeilong is the largest known feathered creature to have lived! And a good reminder that birds are actually living dinosaurs!

27 LIFESIZE books

Maiasaura (my-ah-SORE-ah)

Head to tail: up to 9 metres

Did you know? Maiasaura began life walking on two legs but walked on four when it got older.

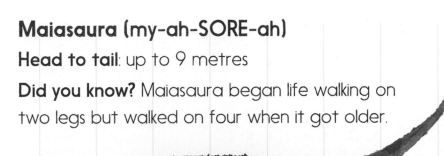

30 LIFESIZE books

Tyrannosaurus rex (tie-RAN-oh-ORE-us rex)

Head to tail: up to 9 metres

Did you know? T. rex had a REALLY big mouth and could eat up to 230 kilograms of meat (about half a horse) in one BIG BITE!

30 LIFESIZE books

Massospondylus (mass-oh-SPON-di-luss)

Head to tail: up to 4 metres

Did you know? Massospondylus had five fingers and a thumb-like digit on its hands.

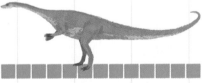

13 LIFESIZE books

Utahraptor (YOU-tah-WRAP-tore)

Head to tail: up to 6 metres

Did you know? Utahraptor had the largest brain for its size of any known dinosaur, so it could have been the smartest!

20 LIFESIZE books

Deinonychus (DIE-non-i-kus)

Head to tail: up to 3 metres

Did you know? It's from studying these dinos that we now know birds are descended from dinosaurs.

10 LIFESIZE books

Microraptor (MIEK-ro-RAP-tor)

Head to tail: up to 0.8 metres

Did you know? Microraptor means 'small thief'.

3 LIFESIZE books